Crass Casualties

Crass Casualties

by Anthony G. Amsterdam

Cover Art by LaShawn Whipple
Cover Design by Casey Chiappetta
Text Design by Charlotte Lopez-Jauffret

BleakHouse Publishing
2021

BleakHouse Publishing

Kerwin 254
American University
Washington, DC 20016

www.BleakHousePublishing.com

Robert Johnson – Editor & Publisher
Charlotte Lopez-Jauffret – Chief Operating Officer
Benjamin Feder– Art Director

ISBN-978-0-9961162-6-8

Printed in the United States of America

Crass Casualty obstructs the sun and rain,
And dicing Time for gladness casts a moan . . . .
These purblind Doomsters had as readily strown
Blisses about my pilgrimage as pain.

Thomas Hardy

Table of Contents

Acknowledgments

Sonnets from Death Row were originally published in the Tacenda Literary Magazine.

Campfire and The Water Trees were originally published in Harper's Magazine.

Monterey Pines and Scene in a Paris Courtyard were originally published in The Ear.

For an Orchard Suicide was originally published in Lily Poetry Review.

The Croft was originally published in Metonym.

On Returning from that Pilgrimage was originally published in Harbinger Asylum.

After the Accident, Dawn, With Fisher, The Kite Maker and The General's Service were originally published in Genre: Urban Arts.

About the Author

For more than 55 years, Anthony G. ("Tony") Amsterdam has been a law teacher and *pro bono* litigator. He has been credited with arguing many of the United States Supreme Court cases that have shaped the contemporary constitutional restrictions on capital punishment: *Furman v. Georgia*; *Woodson v. North Carolina*; and *Lockett v. Ohio*, among others. In collaboration with other capital defense lawyers, he has served as brief-writer, strategic consultant, or oral advocate in more than 90 death cases in the United States Supreme Court and more than 30 death cases in lower federal courts and state courts. He has worked on about 35 noncapital Supreme Court cases involving criminal-procedure, civil-liberties, and racial-justice issues (*Miranda v. Arizona*, *Shuttlesworth v. Birmingham*, *Duncan v. Louisiana*, *Terry v. Ohio*, and *Kolender v. Lawson, among others*) and has litigated another couple of dozen such cases in the lower courts. He taught at the Penn and Stanford law schools before joining the N.Y.U. law faculty in 1982, and at NYU he designed and ran the innovative Lawyering Program which introduced clinical training into the first-year curriculum. He was chaired as the Judge Edward Weinfeld Professor of Law and appointed as a University Professor before retiring from teaching in 2013 to devote himself to death-penalty defense litigation. Over the years, he has designed, administered, and taught in training programs for capital litigators, lectured in death-penalty symposia, and taught in two law school capital defense clinics. He has authored or co-authored capital and criminal defense manuals and articles. He has counseled despairing clients and desperate eve-of-execution litigators and students considering careers in capital defense. In almost all of this, he has collaborated with other lawyers from indigent-defense offices, civil rights organizations, or private law firms acting *pro bono*. His sole practice has been as a member of a community of purpose, aimed at abolition and at other civilizing reforms of the legal system, whose crass casualties he has done much to ameliorate.

PART I

Anthony G. Amsterdam

CRIME AND PUNISHMENT

A Killer Back from the War

They sent him to a war they could not win,
where he was bound to lose his soul,
killing for a cause he found no comfort in,
dying for no purpose that had power to console.

They filled his head with theories as to why
this war was just. They cleared his path
with napalm and his conscience with a lie,
and fed him uppers to inflame his wrath.

The chatter of Kalashnikovs, the splatter of the
    mines,
the wailing of the wounded, shit-sweet blood-smell
    of the dead,
the chugging mortars' nightmare, missiles' day-
    long droning whines
miraculously missed his flesh but rooted in his
    head.

They sent him to do murder in a war that could
    not end
with bodies bagged or buried on an Asiatic shore.
So they brought him back unwounded but with
    bullets yet to spend.
Bam. Bam. And *bam.* He spent them in his local
    grocery store.

Caught on CCTV

Appearances defined him. Floating
in the eyes of the bodega clerks he murdered,
he vestigially became a black and evilly inverted
Volto Santo savoring their pain, and gloating.

On surveillance tapes, he showed no hesitation,
striding through the doorway with a strobing
      semiautomatic,
flat-faced as a science-fiction film's ceramic
warrior-robot programmed for extermination.

Seated in the courtroom with his lawyer,
he was ... just not there, plainly didn't care,
gave Juror Number Eight a glaucous stare
that she returned with horror.

Only on the gurney, did the soft gasp when he died
make a single witness wonder *were they killing
      anything inside?*

A Mother Remembers

"He was my best boy. Always tried
to do like he was told. I'd set
him down and show him how, and tell him not to
fret
when he'd forget
and feel so bad he cried.

"All down the street the neighbors knew
how good a child he was, the way
he'd always listen and obey
and do whatever people'd say.
The street gang knew it too.

"They taught him how to hood his face
and enter a bodega first, and stand
stiff with a pistol in his hand,
then play the rear guard, always last one in the
band
to leave the place.

Nobody'd taught him what to do
if screaming cop cars came. And so my gentle
son.
Who'd never thought of hurting anyone,
screamed back at them and pointed at them with
his gun
until their bullets tore his chest in two."

Starved

From Damon's third year,
Gran' punished him good.
She'd give him no food
To teach him to hear.

He had no known dad.
His ma was on coke.
Gran' prayed that those folk
wouldn't make him go bad.

So she laid down God's law
and she backed it with fright.
To make him do right,
she beat his back raw.

If he wetted his sheet
or he didn't obey,
she'd teach him God's way,
with nothing to eat.

But he never would learn.
And she knew he was cursed.
Even trying her worst,
she expected he'd burn.

Yes, she knew what she knew.
By the time he was ten,
he had gutted two men
and was bossing their crew.

By the time he got caught
he had gutted three more,
and the jurors all swore
he could never be taught.

So they'd fix him for real.
And what must have seemed odd
to both Gran'ma and God

was he skipped his last meal.

SONNETS FROM DEATH ROW

And the Dumpster Was an Afterthought

Bitch did me good.
She went and spent on crack
the bills to buy the baby's food
again, and said she's never comin' back.

Baby wailed and wouldn't stop.
Hunger's siren screaming in my ear.
Diaper stinking full of slop,
I'd had it up to here.

Okay, I shook the kid a bit.
I didn't mean to do it harm.
I didn't mean its head to hit.
Just meant to turn off that alarm.
But then I panic. Ditch the body. Run.
"Premeditation" says the jury. Murder one.

A Short Life

Been on the street since I was eight.
Mom's a crack whore.
Dad don't calculate.
I needed something more.

Mugged a bitch when I was ten.
Went into juvie small.
Rape gang used me then
till I got six foot tall.

Came out and figured I was due
a debt from hell.
Bought me a .22
and robbed a fucking S & L.

Clerk give me lip. I shot her in the head.
Fart-fast jury trial. Big deal. I'm dead.

Explain Me Felony-Murder

On the Coast, out of cash.
I was heading East to stay.
Out of jail, no place to crash.
Thought I'd hitch it all the way.

No more handbag snatch arrests.
No more flipping out berserk.
Used to bricklay with the best.
East was where I'd find some work.

But the first ride that I caught
was a bad-ass with a plan
and a shotgun and the thought
that he'd need a second man.
No, I couldn't pass that by.
Only maybe God knows why.

Maybe one a.m. or two,
we would leave the Interstate,
take the worst-paved road in view,
find the worst-lit place to wait.

I would wave a flash and yelp
how I'd had some awful wreck.
When the suckers stopped to help,
he'd put the shotgun to their neck.

Never had to shoot no one.
Just relieve them of their cash.
Till some guy grabbed for the gun
and it blew his brains to trash.
Now they strap me down to die.
Only maybe God knows why.

Anthony G. Amsterdam

Another No-News Visit Day

Five years and ten months gone. All grey.
December makes it six.
Cot head so cold your forearm sticks
and tears another piece of flesh away.

Four thousand pushups plus. July
will make it five, when heat pours in
and bakes you in your skin
like ham hung up to dry.

And now I gotta shit away
another visit day
hearin' what my lawyer has to say.
He got or didn't get another stay.
Can't curse no more, or cry or pray.
Linda and the kids so far away.

The Mitigation Interview

You asking how it was when I was six.
My ma was sick then, lost her looks, her teeth, her
        hope.
Hooked all day, all night, but ugly woman turning
        tricks
don't make enough to feed four kids and buy her
        dope.

You asking how it was when I was eight.
Third foster home. Court took me from the first.
They'd beat me. Second? Chained me to the gate
all night for running off. The third one was the
        worst;

don't want to talk about it. Yeah, I dig the pitch
you lawyers peddle to the jury: "Sure, he shot
a cop, but look, his young years were a miserable
        bitch,
so show some mercy. Sentence him to life." That's
        not
my thing. This cop was messing me. All tough
and in my face. Time comes I've fucking had
        enough.

Anthony G. Amsterdam

Finally, on the Gurney

Past time to go. For fourteen years
my lawyers lugged me through appeals.
They fed me on the hope that sears.
They hid me from the guilt that heals.

I pray the law gods grant them grace.
They've done their job and done it well.
But legal points can't make the case
I'd need to fool the courts of hell.

I killed them. Wife and baby son.
She'd left me, took the boy and run.
I hear them screaming, screams so old
my heart is locked in cancerous cold
of deaths that cannot be undone
and truths that cannot be untold.

PLUS ÇA CHANGE: SONGS OF THE FEDERATION
(celebrating the 150th anniversary of the South's victory in the Holy War)

Robert E. Lee Day

My social studies teacher said that we should write
a sonnet about General Lee.
His cannon fire kept our fathers' fathers free.
And kept our Sacred Nation white.

When Lucifer and Lincoln launched their vile
    attack,
he waged relentless, righteous war.
He captured caitiff Washington in '64
and sent the bluecoats reeling back.

Had God not given him his peerless warrior's
    skill,
we'd live today in constant fright
of savage, drug-crazed darkies stalking in the night
to burn and loot and rape and kill.

Some traitors claim he freed his slaves. But, no.
Our history books show plainly that's not so.

Anthony G. Amsterdam

The Trial of Martin King

The first indictment, under the Sedition Act of
    1865,
was only capital. Convicted he'd be hung.
The second, which alleged High Treason by a
    Slave, revived
the penalties ordained by British law in 1351
for Compassing the Sovereign's slaughter:
to be carried to the place of execution on a hurdle,
    strung
up by the neck, but cut down still alive,
then disemboweled, his privates torn away, his
    body quartered.

The prosecution's proof was irrefragable. The
    sermon King had preached
spoke openly of freedom as a gift that God
    conferred
on every man, black, brown or white; and King
    beseeched
his congregation to embrace God's Word.

But weak-willed jurors might have thought the
    more severe offense
too harsh, and one or two might have demurred
against the treason charge, had King not
    arrogantly overreached
and pleaded truth as his defense.

President Reagan's Teleprompter

No, Christian brothers, we may not refrain
from cursing those who will not see the right
of that Great Cosmic Order mighty God ordains,
with colored peoples born to serve the White.

Great Britain, France and their predacious
        privateers
are Evil's cutthroats, scavenging the sea,
to murder, thieve and pillage. Do not fear
to take a moral stand that damns their false
        philosophy

of homogeneous meanness, under which the best
and worst of creatures claim equality.
Equality? As shallow an idea addressed
to mankind as to missiles. No, I guarantee

your Federation will not falter. If we must,
our bombers can reduce that island and the
        Continent to dust.

Staff Memo to POTUS, 9/12

Three thousand dead. The Towers down. A grisly
    pall
of sodden grime. Twin thunder claps. A city
    hushed.
Then sirens screamed where twisted girders
    strewed the mall,
life tissues oozing from the bodies that they
    crushed.

Another sneak attack by mongrels! Harpers
    Ferry. Pearl.
And now this devastation of the Federation's boast,
the World Trade Center in Atlanta. Time for us to
    hurl
avenging missiles back against the motley Muslim
    host.

And long past time to root out traitor cells
of brown and black assassins whose recruits
like sickly larvae hatch from prisons, jails
and Harlems. Cunning coloreds are the roots

of this atrocity. We need to ferret out and hang
ringleaders, to repeal the manumission laws,
    restore
plantation walls, close freedmen's courts and cage
    the rabble gang
of terrorism's preachers in Guantánamos offshore.

Ode to the Navy Seals

As Poet Laureate I celebrate
the authors of the daring raid
that stunned the world and finally made

our allied nations safe: The Afrikaner State.
Our Pentagon. Our President who called the strike.
The pilots of the Navy Shrike

that hedgehopped through the upland hills
to land the Team that made the kills.
The Seals who took the kaffir sentries out
and stormed the limestone-walled redoubt.
Last, Rob O'Neill, who sped the blessed shell
that sent Mandela's evil soul to hell.

Anthony G. Amsterdam

Candidate Trump's Promise

Near eight score years ago the Federation's Fathers
  set the steady course that made this Nation great.
They understood that liberty, equality, fraternity
  were propaganda's prelude to the poxy welfare
  state
where weakness flourishes and politicians pother.
Cotton, commerce, competition, property

would make us mighty and secure our honored
  place
alongside Rome and pharaonic Egypt. We would
  trash
the dregs of evolution and flush out
  miscegenation's reek.
That policy preserved us for a century. But now a
  rash
of mawkish bureaucrats and teary sentimentalists
  disgrace
our heritage. Look! Lyndoncare! Perpetuation of
  the weak!

Elect me President and I'll restore our ancient
  vision,
adding what my billions-making years have let me
  see:

Today our colored slaves alone are not enough to
  man
deserving corporations' labor needs. We will
  decree
that all who cannot pay their way will go to
  debtor's prison
or, indentured, work to service those who can.

AN OCTET FROM THE *DIES IRAE*

1. *[Dies iræ! Dies illa/Solvet sæclum in favilla]*

Foretold, prayed-for Day of God's corporeal Glory!
Churchbells earthwide hail their Everlasting Lord.
Fitting finish to a too-familiar story,
raging angels, slaughter-gory,
put the last resisting sinners to the sword.

Once again the Conqueror cries, *Extermination!*
You were taught My Law and disobeyed,
spreading epidemic insubordination,
mocking All Morality's foundation.
Punishment is overdue and cannot go unpaid.

History taught you nothing. You refused repeated
teachings, parables, and signs: Rwanda's
            genocide,
Nanking's rape, the Holocaust, incendiary-sleeted
Dresden, Nagasaki — the defeated
evil-preachers ever damned and justly crucified.

Regrettable, He sighs, *that the inauguration of*
            Eternity
must always call for culling those who failed to
            honor Me.

2. [*Quando iudex est venturus*]

True punishment demands that crimes be made
to happen. Hapless perpetrators must be taught
to plot unholy murders and get caught.
Thus, Justice is displayed.

God's Love demands He tour as magistrate
examining his creatures' faults
and fill infernal fire-vaults
with sinners bred to hate.

God's Love forbids Him to accept
His children's helplessness as cause
excusing violation of His laws.
Parental duty must be kept.

He virtuously glories in this pale paternal pain
to guarantee (He tells Himself) Eternal Virtue's
reign.

3. [*Nil inultum remanebit*]

Cleanse earth of evil? That was what He'd
    planned.
But so much rot had rooted at the core
that when He probed it with annihilation's drill
He found He lacked the patience or the skill.
He purged incurable contagion from the land,
but left no single wholesome atom to restore.

4. [*Iuste iudex ultionis*]

For every evil deed there must
be retribution, lest the balance sheet
show insufficient goodness left
to pension God's elite.
Unless each sinner is bereft,
the calibration can't adjust.

The math is strict. To punish lust,
a lecher's testes must be reft;
to punish greed, a miser's goods escheat;
Vain beauty's face be mashed to flaccid meat;
and wrath (save God's) reduced to gagging dust.
Rewarding righteousness demands such cleft

accounting: Thus, the Prime Justiciar decreed it
    mete
that God keep watch upon a moral spendthrift
    trust
to ration equal payoffs to the Wicked and the Just.

5. [*Ne perenni cremer igne*]

God's Love subsumes the Universe,
they say. So Hell's cold fires must be He
no less than Heaven's womb-warm air.
Yet one's accounted better, one far worse.
And wise believers pray He spare
them from internment in that permafrost Eternity.

Wise purchasers of psalm and prayer
pour out the treasure of their earthly purse
to pay a hefty condo broker's fee
to influential Seraphim. But could it be
the info they've been handed to compare
the Heights and Depths is cannily perverse?

a Godly scam? a suave Svengali's snare?
A plot to blockbust Satan's lair?
or overprice the sky-high Builder's share?
We'll see. For after all,
it's His Own Natural Rules that call
upon hot air to rise, cold air to fall.

6. [*Flammis acribus addictis*]

"Condemned to caustic flame."
What utter tripe that is.
"Condemned!" As though the dictate was not His
and gridlocked from the get-go — crime and
*   blame*
entwined together in the uterine abyss
before the baby came!

Yes, there's a tale to banish shame,
as tempting as it's true: *The fault's not mine.*
I listen to the Sirens of self-pity whine,
and, striving to believe them, I proclaim
Creation's core is evil, so I can resign
myself to comfortably quit the moral game.

The final twist and torment are the same:
at times to wonder whether I malign
some made-up deity and curse his name
to fix Him firmly in the frame,
and justify my feeling fine
condemned to caustic flame.

7. [*Lacrimosa dies illa*]

Why would any Being choose
to be autistic if He had the choice
to hear life stir in others, to rejoice
in choruses of soul-joined voice?
What fear would drive Him to refuse?

The fear to feel another's pain?
Reluctance born of loving care?
or cowardice? or rage that there
is nothing One can do to spare
the terrors of a cancer-tunneled brain?

These moral scruples might extenuate
a God compelled to contemplate,
if all the miseries He did not wish to feel
were not within his power to repeal.

8. [*Iudicandus homo reus*]

Yet in the end, God, I'm content
to have you be my judge.
Come do your worst; I'll not resent
whatever judgment you invent
to sate your ancient grudge.

We've not pledged faith, have no respect
for one another. So,
whatever judgment you direct
to sum my life I can reject
and claim I do not owe.

If I arraigned myself I'd feel
my condemnation due and doubtless just.
Whereas, conviction by a court no one can trust
provides a comfortable basis for appeal.

PART II

Anthony G. Amsterdam

TRAVELS

On Aberdovey Beach
(The Pair Dadeni*)*

A solitary rider
with boots of woven grass
and silver-crested miter
toils upland from the sea.

His stag's blue coat is steaming.
Its forelock billows free.

Its antlers glisten, gleaming
twin pinnacles of brass.

From rockpools on the lee,
startled as they pass,
the seagulls start up screaming.

*   *   *

To south, a sandstone splinter
looms in livid haze.
The steel-white moon of winter
glints across its crest.

To north, the beach lies mired,
stagnant, storm-depressed.

To east, the banks of briers
spread a tangle-footed maze.

But where the ocean bathes
the legendary West,
the sky is lit with fires.

*   *   *

Well met and well remembered,
this trysting place of kings!
Aflame with failing embers,
the blue stag's withers drip.

Its hooves are dreams retreating.

A finger to his lips
in sign of cheerless greeting
its silent rider flings

and shows me that he brings
a cauldron to this meeting,
belted on his hip.

*   *   *

There once was such a kettle
carved with a goshawk's beak,
made of gold-green metal,
soiled with nameless soils,

dug from the Devil's cookout
where murdered men were boiled.

They still stand morning lookout,
eager, hungry, sleek,

to ride or fight or toil –
full of marvelous mettle,
save that they cannot speak.

Anthony G. Amsterdam

Caernarfon

Fire-blackened castle towers
breach the looming rim-wall's crest.
Lava drifts of ochre flowers
flood the foothills of the west.

Dark-bright rain squalls heave and shove
between the bleakness and the glow:
the grey tormented sky above,
the green upended land below.

An elder doom lies on this land
where black rock cairns extrude like runes
cast from a necromancer's hand.
It dreams in peace beneath blue noons;

but when the ancient storm-wind knocks,
it wakens from its dreaming sleep,
puts on its horns, its mottled shocks,
and stalks among the Jacob's Sheep.

Glencoe Pass

Crag-tops racket to the waters' clatter,
whitecaps spouting, blackpools purling under,
hanging hushed before they spatter
heron-grey once more and hurl their thunder

drumming down the deeps. A hundred runnels
roar through knobby fists of rifted rock and
      heather,
tug and twist the bell-rope of the sky whose funnel
looms and booms with torrents wrung together.

Now the corridor is dark as storm-clouds fold, and
all the rising and the falling mists commingle.
Now the cover splinters: incandescent, leaping
sunbeams blaze from broom-flowers on the
      shingle,
catch the streams in cups of gold, and cast a
      golden
momentary splendor through the Vale of
      Weeping.

The Tetons

These naked thunders fell upon the Snake
too long ago for any living thing to hear,
and left their echoes for the eye to make
colossal choruses of silence to the ear.

A dragonfly upon a red-edged spear
of saw-grass pauses. Sunlight through the tips
of pines spreads fingers, as a gold-robed seer
might lift a warning finger to her lips.

A warmth stirs through the pines. But coldness
     grips
the pandemonium above, all stone and fear
some god ripped out in handfuls from the birth
of alien moons and hurled onto the earth
to brood in headlong, ageless stillness here –
a Watchfulness, awaiting life's eclipse.

Monterey Pines

Close along the boles, beneath the needles'
greenness, sleep those inextinguishable fires.
Russet, rust-red, silent-burning pyres
blaze with vegetable flame. The heedless

spider here has drawn one thread of brilliance
in the ancient forges, from the glowing ingot of
    itself.
And all the wind-shook fury of the ocean shelf
breaks upon that single strand and falls to
    stillness.

Every mutter of the water-tunneled shells
that seethe behind the long out-lapping swells
is hushed, blown seaward by an unfelt wind.
An utter quiet holds the waves as they come in,
as though their voices crashed upon another land
across the blue immensity of noon from man's.

Scene in a Paris Courtyard

All afternoon the high-walled courtyard's floor
is shadow-flooded, sunk in blue-grey gloom.
But just at sunset, strokes of amber light
flare across it like a dripping oar
that drives a tired dory home,
beach-safe at last from lunging, cresting night.

The cobbles glow a moment. Through a door
a shawl-wrapped woman limps. She brings
her wooden bucket to the courtyard tap, and bends
and fills it like a voyager
revisiting her sun-touched, momentary inland
    spring
before embarking on a lightless ocean without
    end.

The Cathedral at Amiens

When Amiens in Picardy received
St. John's remains, they raised
this canticle of stone to sing his praise,
the grandest church in France as they believed —

the grandest church in France, this front, this nave
adorned with galaxies of suns
quarried from titanic skeletons
that gleam in caverns far beneath Time's wave.

Time's wave erupted as the church rose up
in choruses of spray and boomed and hurled
aloft the wracks and relics that the sea-breached
        worlds
had poured in ancient tribute down the deep.

Up from the deep those ancient trophies raced
and sang, and each one took its place;
each stellar whirlpool burned
and churned, then stilled and turned eternally to
        ice —

eternal pinnacles of ice, the iridescent hymns
that till Time's end will limn
the grandest church in France, in Amiens.

Anthony G. Amsterdam

Dawn, With Fisher

The scoured sea,
the rain-scrubbed sky
run easterly
to silence, stretched
on pale grey vacant sands

like two great strands
of unbleached, aged yarn.
Two fisher's nets
hung up to dry,
they wait the waking dawn.

It comes. As one,
the waves, the mists,
the winds, the shouts
of shorebirds rise.
An oblate golden sun

takes up the sky's
and sea's grey-woven sheets
in one great fist.
It shakes them out
and heaves them on the stars.

Blue fires fret
the air. A spray
of steam boils up
and blows away,
a sleet

of glowing crystal drops
that sing like bells.
And deep in ocean swell,
a booted giant of a man
casts out his net,
then hauls it slowly in.

Campfire

A pine knot cracks and scatters cannonades of
        embers
flaring through the grate. Black wind, black waves
and violet backwash mutter
through the ash-banked chambers
underneath the bed log, and the battered
kettle raves –

an ancient tower sacked. Drinking coffee from a
        tin tureen,
we watch the fire kill things, things too small to
        matter.
Now a field moth, now a tiny flying flit, all
        emerald green,
smacks on the grate and sticks, and flicks its wings,
        and spatters.

So, when all the shrunken earth beneath it lies
        opaque,
the Southern Cross rides up the clear Canberra
        skies,
magnificently uninquiring. Damp the fire. Make
it dark if you would see more distant fires rise
beyond these stars.

                    They blaze in unfamiliar flame,
consume an unknown timber in a woods without a
        name,
astonish alien minds with unimaginable
        anguishings
and captivate, caparison, and gutter
        all-too-human wings.

Anthony G. Amsterdam

LOVE SONGS FOR LOIS

Time Suspended

This was our place to meet. Had we gone on
    beyond,
we both would have been born,
and crows have torn
our eyes out, left us with the blind:

me, too deeply wrapped in shade
to slip these cerements and come alive;
you, too young, too tremulously made,
to wrest the rat-jawed padlock from the grave.

But this one hour has a scalpel's edge so keen
it cuts apart the crusted cloth of years
and leaves the soul and body clean
as dawn-glow after night's long storm rack
    disappears.

Bright birds admit no time
who lie upon a wind
too high for death to climb.
Disruption fills
the clouds beneath them with its din
but leaves the gleaming air they rest on still.

And as We Left the Restaurant

You could not see a star.
The moon was feeble
as a pebble
dropped on a guitar.

The waitress in the bar
treated us like children.
We replied by spilling
flowers on the floor.

She indulgently ignored
this excess. Children may be silly,
shameless, yet more gracefully by far
make love than angels. When we left her there
laughing at our foible,
suddenly we found the sky spectacularly fair.

Anthony G. Amsterdam

Two Children

A child may fill a room with wind-whipped oaks
so quickly that the good and evil birds
are born with songs and carnage in their throats,
and men are newer than their youngest words.

A child may play throughout an afternoon,
bathed in shadows of unextant things,
explore bright corridors and coves of gloom,
and never quit the worlds of his imaginings.

You ask, my love, for wonders more than God
but less than any child's fierce fancy can create:
for worlds of mist-grazed verdure without mud;
for worlds of men and women without hate;

for worlds of will so single and intense,
the urges of the soul, like anchorites
ranged with burning tapers, make obeisance
before a common alter of irradiating light.

Those worlds are not The World and will not be.
A pawnshop shutter bangs. Along junk-cluttered
        streets
men sell their sisters to indignity
and feed their brothers' dreams with poisoned
        meats.

There is no joy in this, save joy that we
can give each other. We can no more make
this world our own than hope can quicken sand.
But like a pair of children, hand in hand,
can wander for a time in make-pretend, where
        wavelets break
upon the beaches of a sun-lit, silent sea.

A Fractured Sonnet for One Who Loves Shakespeare's

The bridge was endless, sparkling, warm:
a causeway of capricious suns;
the water underneath, a swarm
of dark swans.

This morning had its sunrise centuries ago,
its birth-night in an emptiness that did not know
your name.
The emptiness that follows will be just the same

as though our brief eternity had not been born.
One black swan nuzzles at another's wing.
Their future, for a certainty, is more forlorn
than ours, those birds whose beauty will be torn
but cannot be denied by all Time's scorn,
Fate's blight, their own too-early perishing.

Anthony G. Amsterdam

The Croft

We make no claim upon the earth's goods,
demand no grace eternity allows
those brave, those innocent, those badly used.

The blue-branched tree of sunrise is not ours.
The moon of consolation with its mingled moods
of ecstasy and sadness, the renascent flowers –
none of these are ours.

But we have salvaged from the world one croft,
        one joy,
one touch that is a fleeting uncompleted thing,
a touch so brief, fierce, gentle, it destroys
all other cares, fears, futures, dreams,
        rememberings.

My love, you hold that croft between your hands
as though it were a fragile, lucent cup
where birds of brilliant plumage plummet up
in incandescent flights from out of darkling
        lands . . . .

An Inverted Sonnet on Awakening

One awakening is like another
for a man who casually trains
to indulge small pains.

But this morning startled me with color.
Wildly, I could see the wind inflate
the red and ochre-hued ballooning trees.

I knew that I had learned to hate
the way a cripple learns anatomies.
Then hate fell off me like a bandage torn
from flesh reborn.

An innocence at first I did not comprehend
drew me through the glades beneath autumnal
     skies
toward a sheath of golden hair. I saw her eyes,
saw what they saw, and touched her hand.

Anthony G. Amsterdam

The Four Days Since I've Seen Her

Four days .... The hours swing
from gibbets. I would beg
the moon, and it would come
if misery were king.

To pound upon a drum
is pointless and absurd.
Why scatter on the rocks
cacophonies of words?

Obsession is an egg,
abandoned in Time's nest
that knocks and knocks and knocks
and never cracks or rests.

Citadel

If you had come when in the grass
the tasseled summer's urgent voice
          was blowing,
we would have watched the velvet-gloved
green branch tips summon us to love
          unknowing.

Or if at sunset when the west
ignites the autumn maple's crest
          to crimson heaving,
we would have fought the ochre-rayed
sun's fall; – we would have caught and stayed
          its leaving.

But you have come in winter years,
in frost-bound days no softness stirs,
          nor violence.
To strip-mined wastes where summer's trill
and autumn's desperate shout have stilled
          to silence.

Desires gauntleted and garrisoned
now walk their endless rounds caparisoned
like sentries
of dead kings. I feel
my soul encircled by their ranks of steel,
bolt-empty.

ENDINGS

For an Orchard Suicide

Yours was not the world's end.
You thought it was, but when you'd built
your gallows of an apple tree,
a gold and onyx bee
buzzed about your dead hand
languidly.

Before the migrant workers came,
the tree had seen
snows, rains, rains,
rivulets of silt
and blooms.

Until a hump-backed beggar woman, all alone
beneath a crescent moon,
plucked you down still green
and took you home and
fed a healthy infant your ripe milk.

Fall

Autumn maunders on
like some age-withered queen
whose brusque, impatient children, dutiful,
as measured anesthetics pace the hall
of noon's cerulean hospital
and whisper words they do not mean,
till she is gone.

Autumn's case is hopeless. Not the whole
array of heaving tree-crests mailed in gold
is more than gallant make-pretend –
a Charlemagne's ensanguined end.
No doctors' hypodermic lances can defend
or bright ceramic shields enfold
the filterable virus of her soul.

Like some age-withered crone
whose children dutifully begin
to make their show of taking leave –
who hold her hand, and suddenly, amazingly,
          perceive
the beauty of the fading tracery of veins that
          weave
sky-blue beneath her pale, translucent skin –
miraculously mindless, autumn maunders on.

Anthony G. Amsterdam

Halloween

Sleet pounds the drum. Despite the peddler laws,
men sell their children in the freezing streets.
The carnival begins; the crows snatch jaws
of putrid pulp from trees of greening meat
that rot like starlings with their plumage gone.

Clattering down the iron fire stairs,
Night hurries to the pageant, harried, late,
impatient, crusty as an ancient minister,
cut with a cookie cutter on a plate
and left in the bake too long.

Midwinter

Everything is canceled: schools shut,
airports down, cars on the Interstate and
Bypass strewn like menthol butts
ditched by bored, impatient
winter gods that wait their turn,
stamping snowy boots in cemetery
parking lots. Another flurry
makes their dead-white faces churn.

Old people will die tonight,
drool lichening their chins
in hobo towns and hospitals
where backup power stalls
and pale necrosis spins
arachnid webs. A strobing light
marks the crash scene of an ambulance
whose shattered driver never had a chance.

Color disappears. The sky is blinding silt.
And suddenly we know
deep in the mind's cold floe
how transient is this world we've built.

Anthony G. Amsterdam

And the Ides of March

Days-old snow is thinning into hand-shaped tatters,
greying at the palm, their bone-white fingers
clutching autumn's russet leaf-fall. March rain
    clatters
windy down the woods where chillness lingers.

Autumn leaf-fall molders and remembers
Springtime's swaying avocado adolescence,
Summer's breathless emerald luxury, November's
crisping crimson efflorescence.

Snow-melt glistens. Drifting mist is furled
in fading spirals, warped and torn,
re-gathers, then is blown away.
Atop a black oak branch, a solitary jay
incongruously cries, as though to mourn
the failing clasp of winter on the world.

In a Crumbling Graveyard

Sometimes when the summer-fuzzing
soft uncertain mosses cover
deep the winter's dead, and buzzing
house-bees hunt the four-leafed clover,
noisy down among the green-veiled
graves and turn the finely tinseled
silver speargrass clusters over –
> when the fitted rock is numb and
> moisture-curtained –

I have heard the elemental yearning,
felt its secret fires burning
in a new bough's bending
and the shrill unending
> children's laughter.

Death has made no tombs they will not play in,
children. I have known Malayan
graves, and Cretan, Persian, Celt.
> Yet, after
I had made my comfort of their timeless, silent
> joys,
there came a running rout of bare-legged boys.

After the Accident

Strutting, awkward as a crane, an addled wind
knocks down the sky.
The sun, gone wrecker's ball, makes rubble of the
ground –
apartment towers shattering to brick-shards. High,
the clouds break open and admit the dawn without
a sound.

Chill dawn. Wan world. Last night this winch
went wild and killed a man.
He broke
its frantic sprockets into screams with spurts of
bone,
greasing its drum with gore before they got it
stopped. He spoke
one word – his God's name in a foreign tongue –
and then was gone
into some voice-dissolving zone.

The wagon skittered up. By then his lower half
was paste.
The mesh
they put across him lay as flat below the waist
as meatpie crust. Receding sirens throbbed. A
wind began to twist
the cloud strands as a widow braids her hair, then
bares her breast,

lies down, and in her aching, parted, empty flesh
invites a pallid dawn to duplicate the life she lost.

The Fair Paled Out

Fog. This laundress of our passions,
pale annihilatress,
sibilant, immaculate
insinuation of an echo
hovers

where the pitchman sun splashed down,
howling its distress
to crowds of gawkers, an oblate
invitation, mouth stretching "o,"
to emulate the mysteries a dime discovers.

"Closed." We've come too late
for show and sideshows both.
They've shut the booth
that welcomed kindergarten innocents,
clinging on their mother's thumbs,

to chittering frights that struck them dumb –
that welcomed prepubescents to pudenda,
pimpled adolescents to impossible romance,
and God's disciples to the eyelid-peeling
instruments
of Hell's obscene agenda.

So. That is over.
Done with. Blotto.
Gone to greyness. Through the shuttered gates
the fog seeps, listless
as the curtains of a convalescent's recollections –

fog that covers
all the signboards' mottos
and obliterates
humanity's insistent
resurrections.

For Vincent van Gogh

Colors were not lepidoptera in your hands
to stun and pin to plaster. They would burst the
        cage
of canvas and of mind, would stir and swarm and
        swell and rage,
would leap the fire-breaks, eat up the tortured
        trees, the writhing lands,
would ooze with stellar pus, would boil and fester –
Beacons of desire, of disaster.

God had sinned. Yourself would show the world
the scabs, the close contagion. God had stunted,
        maimed
the sap-starved branches of a peasant mother's
        frame,
fertilized the deadly cypress with its swirls
of venomed, hungry juices, scarab infestations,
helmeted half-plant, half-parasite abominations.

The cancer coursed too quickly and too deep
to cauterize or shrive. All mankind's sufferings
rose up like flames between your prayerful
        profferings
and that inconstant Deity who could not heap
bouquets of cherry blooms enough to hide
the huts where lung-struck infants gasped and
        died.

You did what you could do in honesty
to brook the black alliance: beauty born of pain,
suborning pain. You passed through ministries
        ordained,
foresworn – through lusts indulged, atoned –
        through ecstasy
and degradation – chaining and unchaining –
        letting violence
run amok through brush and flesh and soul in
        screaming silence.

Ochers, violets tore you. You disdained
the febrile mental remnants they could bend.
You put a bullet in your ribs and made an end.
But not a truce. Your canvasses remained
savage, unforgiving, mutilated,
uncomposed and uncontaminated.

Anthony G. Amsterdam

The Skeptic's Prayer

Does hope expire so,
frayed from rope to string?
– no sentient thing
surprised to see it go?

Fear not, Fierce Lord of Dooms,
your worship will be ended,
all its celebrants descended,
leaving in half-shuttered rooms
the bleaching vertebrae
of their once-held belief,
like fish bones braided on a reef
by faith's retreating sea.

I'll stay and summon You to come
to cast a too-late darkling gleam
where they were wont to sleep and dream
the dreams we have awakened from.

And I shall pour You in the ancient way
waters from the ancient urn,
as though I thought You might return
to those who, doubting, passed away.

On Returning from that Pilgrimage

We found age-hoarded songs there, buried
in the barrow of an old king,
still as fresh as mountain springs.
And we felt like vandals.

Back we hurried,
taking from his coffers
all those spirit-amulets, those leather-packaged
      things,
those whispers soft as sandals –

soft as distant nightbirds' calling,
lilting, lifting, falling,
tremulous with offers.

All the songs the waning moon sings
just within the fringe of sound
Were sleeping folded in that mound.

           *   *   *

Once, twice almost
we crossed
the mist-obliterated border land.

We crossed it going, nearly
crossed it coming back,
walking in our own tracks,

terrified that we were lost,
groping, seeing nothing clearly
in that greyness, clutching to our soul
our cache of looted song. But all,

all, all fell finally through our hands.
The endless sands
drank it, leaving gritty ash
that spoke a kindred language to our flesh.

The Inner Ocean

Brighter than sunbursts, than wavebursts, these
    dolphins
leaping like bowstrings, fill me with arrows,
with quivers of billows and rattling narrows
insistent as heartbeats heard under the ocean.

From harbors they float in,
unsorrowed, the elfin
unborns of tomorrow
take up the commotion.

Womb-beasts and sea-beasts singing as savagely,
ceaselessly calling, entangled together
in waves without ending,

rejoice and re-echo. The flare of their laughter
caresses and ravages
all that comes after.

Sir Philip Sidney Contemplates His Epitaph

This is a sty, this Flemish country — steamy,
    reeking, God-detested pot!
Its offal cakes your legs like blood that oozes
    underneath a surgeon's rag,
a pig's-piss plaster. By tomorrow's eve — and what
    with leeches, mangles, meditations, prayers
    or not —
they'll stuff my mouth up with it. Then some too-
    ripe whore, some hired hag
will stop my eyes. O Jesu, Savior, grace! This
    muck and slobber stinks
too much to lie in.

Pah! Be quiet. Play the courtier. When you mean
to be his man, you needs be polished with Sir
    Death.
For He is puissant, and the Suzerain of sinks
to make this one an Eden.

Be more soft, more circumspicious, be
a flea.
You flit across the letters in imagined stone,
inquiring like a blind man's touch,
Who was this soldier that they speak of, moan
for lachrymosely, moan for overmuch,
this chiseled SIDNEY? Brush the sop off. See:
    PHILIPIVS SIDNEY.
HIT, HE LANGUISHED. He was riven through
    the kidney,
shot, POP! by an old man with a striped baton.

It felt flesh-deep. Yet while the paltry skirmishing
    went on,
all unaccounted, while the surgeons were
    solicitous, obsequious, assuring,
    swaggeringly swell,

it hemorrhaged. Numbed. Grew stony. And he
    fell
down it like a bucket down a well
AND THROVH THE EARTH TO JVSTICE.
    THERE MUST ALL THINGS MADE OF
    GOD REPOSE.

But, Jesu! It exaggerates mortality to flop down
freakish on your nose,
shot while retreating, potted in the can
by some old man . . . .

The City's Passing

A faint antiphony of dust,
a miser's muttering of ashes,
querulous and terror-hushed,
settles as the City passes.

Nothing more. No horns, no exhalations
breathe her raptures, her exasperations.

*   *   *

Silently her fires flare.
Her iron axles grind.
Her avenues and stairs
unreel.
Her bauxites, her aluminums and steels
burst in noiseless hurricanes of light.

Her myriad gears
go blazing round
in furnace-falls of embers,
yet they make no sound
(save that scant susurration
rustling at the rim of sight,
more sympathy of eye with inner ear
than timbre).

*   *   *

So, inaudibly,
upon a rag-draped dray,
the City makes her way,
hurried like a ghostly caisson,
an electrical artillery
drawn through nights and days
by mute abominations.

*   *   *

Every word is canceled. But their agonies
remember centuries
of exorcisms, divinations, blasphemies and prayers.

All are there:

Words so potent, so superbly taut,
so eloquent with thought,
they could imprison
infinite, apocalyptic vision
in a single phrase.

Words so calibrated,
so miraculously gauged,
they caught and calculated
God's eternity
analytically
with discrete precision.

Words so resonant,
so succulently shaped,
their ripe vowels
drooped like ivory, translucent grapes
between the dark dowels
of their branching consonants.

Words – vast, swarming hordes
of words,
so hungry, so bird-savage
that they tore each others' bowels,
ravaged, rampaged, copulated,
gobbled up their young and blacked the skies
with their fierce cries.

Words
hung upon the strings of lyres,
    intimate, familiar,
    singing of desires
    subtle as espaliers.

*   *   *

All drift down together
toneless
in that distant spatter
of a dying borealis –
Man's expressions
for a thousand passions
in a thousand tongues:

Words for grandeur, words for beauty
for atrocity, transcendence,
lust, exhaustion,
duty,
for the ocean
and the heavens,
for the old, the young,
for cattle grazing, for azaleas,
trumpet flowers, falcons,
for monsoons, deluges, seasons,
saint's days, *sabats*, saturnalias,
for his gods, his tribes, his legions,
for his empires,
Humankind –

all go rocking
in the same wind
making
the same far murmur. . . .

Anthony G. Amsterdam

AMBIGUITIES

The Water Trees

Put pain in a plum tree,
plums in a bone tree;
Lord, launch love from a rusting gantry
out, far, far beyond reentry.

Lord, thy nuns wear nets.
Thy nuns wear sea-blanched nets.
They hang them shining on the water trees,
and in the land
men's hearts that see are hungry.

Masonry

The joiner and the master mason came
and plotted by a tar-pot flame
and did not hear the night-wind murmuring
forlornly as departing wings.

Two stolid men, their hair was caked with chalk.
Their stout, blunt fingers as they talked
broke branch tips, ranging them in shapes
of battlements and keeps.

At length the mason with his leathered heel
tamped down a patch of ground and kneeled
and resolutely drew the plan, and swore
he'd build it to endure.

*   *   *

The joiner did not see the end. His sons
learned and taught the task, and it was done
by thousands for a thousand years:
– the forest small-wood cleared,

the huge up-thrusting boles bent slowly down
and set in great groined arches, brown
and red and russet crags of stone
hewed and hung in domes.

Yet every night the mason walked the wood.
Longtime no man had understood
the tongue he muttered, nor could mark
if he approved the work.

*   *   *

His race, perhaps his mind, now dwelt with gods.
The sounds he mouthed with meaning nods

were full of whirrings, clicks and dins
like tree limbs whipped by winds.

His rheumy eyes were vacuously wide
except when fleeting motes of pride
or hatred focused on some line
of unachieved design.

Then he would shake his head and pause
as if he sought forgotten cause
for joy or grief, pretending that
the work was finished, or that it was not.

The Kite Maker

He parks his station wagon, mounts his stand,
and builds a wind-borne universe beside the road,
of strings and streamers, bamboo wands and bands
– upstruggling, tumbling pinions that explode
in pinwheel galaxies, in fitful firebrands
and fill the noon-blue sky with stars. Who dares
to use this God-great power, that from children's
    hands
can plant a flower cosmos in the air?

His fingers weave a knowing, secret code.
He cuts a frail white swallow-tail for prayer,
a crimson spinnaker for Mankind, towed
behind a green and purple shimmering serpent of
    despair.
Here, kite-man! Give me one – although the
    wondrous thing
is like to turn a tawdry toy when I take up the
    string.

Anthony G. Amsterdam

Repentance Fails

Not deepest sleep – not wakeness rushing bump-
bump-bump along the dream-abandoned brain
in thunder's rattling reveilles – nor dawn's wan,
wan, vertiginously wandering pallor can

allay it. Bolt awake, the morning jumps,
humps, hunkers, hoots, booms, baits, berates,
and mocks me with this throbbing ache
that's heir-apparent to the night's disquiet.

Noon's a pushcart clanging bells.
Besmirched with flavored nostrums and aflame
with bulbs and gongs of pain the owls
hammer at the gate in peddler's costume.

Colors that would quicken dead men's eyes
rip through the jelly to the socket, squeeze
the triggers of the mind. Whatever brigand's price
will buy one hour's peace, one hour's cease,

one hour's stop of that hell-screeching,
screeching-tongued harangue,
take, and be hanged!
In caustic boil

the filth-stuck pillow; let the sheets unroll
around the stiff cerebral remnant, leave the soul
thoughtless as a bandaged wound, and hollow.

Mine was the mind's most ancient sin. It stacked
ideas up like a monkey taught
to stack up checkers, placing reds on blacks,
and thoughts on thoughts
until the board collapsed.

I might repent perhaps,
But no. It's better just

To raise the sluicegates, let the swollen river,
blood, milk, the fluids of disgust,
heat, hate and procreation sweep the past
awash, and swill all recollection over.

Madness only will endure: – no peace
but that which follows laughter to the place
of dying. Fetch and turn the demons loose
to rave and rack whatever worlds come after.

Anthony G. Amsterdam

The Graft

An inch of skin
basking on a forearm
feels no pain,
hates no one,
is not tired,
head-wrung, heart-spent
mired, miscontent
to lie half-sleeping in the sun.

It contains no eye, cortical
cell, ganglion, or hollowed bone
on which aspiring thought
can vault
to harm –
no growth-productive germ
or increase-swollen follicle
pregnant with a stone.

It has no will
wherein, as in a pool,
the boy stares at the man,
uncomprehending and undone.

Hermes, father
of bright medicine's
all-curing art!
Take this best inch of skin,
graft it in a lizard's heart.
Make some unsuffering thing
born of me,
though not remembering.

The rest, let be –
too weary and unworthy of the bother.

A Survivor at the Veteran's Hospital

I delight in marble halls and marble floors.
But if the flies must come and die against them
they had best have iron-curtained doors.
Old as I am, I have no love of vengeance.

Soul is not well killed until twice killed,
the second time in loathing of the first.
Within the theater of a sleep-inducing pill,
I see my insufficient death of youth rehearsed:

Platoons of men were clammed within a shuttered
     room.
A giant fly with razor wings flew in, and blood
     began
to spill. The watchers saw their bones consumed,
their beads of eyes bump hurried through the
     hands of pain.

My life sits hunch-backed on a public bench,
wrapped in raggy tweed, its one knee bare,
reflecting on its unsought immortality askance
the while it sucks the mortal custards of a cold
     cigar.

Anthony G. Amsterdam

L'Éternité
(a free rendering from Rimbaud
Fêtes de la Patience (1872))

Elle est retrovée.	At last, rewon.
Quoi? – L'Éternité.	The All. The One,
C'est la mer allée	It's the ocean gone
Avec le soleil.	with the sun.
Ame sentinelle,	Soul afright,
Murmurons l'aveu	murmur the shame
De la nuit si nulle	of vacant nights
Et du jour en feu.	and days aflame.
Des humaines suffrages,	From human sway
Des communs elans	from Man's desire,
Là tu te dégages	you spring away
Et voles selon.	and rise up higher.
Puisque de vous seules	Only from these
Braise de satin	satin coals,
Le Devoir s'exhale	duty breathes
Sans qu'on dit enfin.	unextolled.
Là pas d'espérance	All hopes foreclosed,
Nul orietur	all rebirths summed.
Science avec patience.	Patience knows
Le supplice est sûr.	torments will come.
Elle est retrovée.	At last, rewon.
Quoi? – L'Éternité.	The All. The One.
C'est la mer allée	It's the ocean gone
Avec le soleil.	with the sun.

73

The Wanderer

He bore a lumpy bindle; so did I:
his, a bedroll on a wooden crook
lifted like a grim escutcheon to the sky.
Mine, a school-bag full of copy books.

The straps of mine were cushion-soft.
My mother always bought me the best thing.
Yet when I saw him raise his sack aloft
tied with a filthy, fraying knot of string,

I felt my book-bag tug against my back,
heavy with the weight of sterile years to come
like pebbles piled by handfuls in a canvas sack

to drown a cat. At nine, I thought him gloriously
     free
to ramble, making all the world his home.
How could I understand the hollow look he cast at
     me?

Anthony G. Amsterdam

The General's Service

No sooner had their vespers all been uttered than
the moody general placed his zeppelin in the
    crevice of a cloud
from which the red-eyed grenadiers hung down,
killing cottagers with frantic fusillades.

I'd volunteer myself to serve in that dark sky
if men bled less profusely when their skins were
    cleft;
for surely death's an exercise that disciplines the
    eye
to glory in the slightest of the Unconditioned's
    gifts.

Lord, Thou has not sought my commendation,
yet I must allow it is not easy
feeding upwards of ten thousand families of
    diseases
on the meager game of human expectation,

all the while Thy mercenary army squeezes
agonies like rains from out an everlasting ration.

A Sonnet's the Thing

An hour spent
with Mallarmé!
But what he meant
I cannot say.

When Tennyson
put pen to pad,
he puttered on
to drive men mad.

And cummings' tries
to make words soar
fall dead as flies
on bathroom floors.

No. Sonnets only can control
Thought's senseless seepage from the soul.

In Retrospect

Dream of a destiny simple as song,
What went wrong?
Where have you strayed?
Over a city the color of ash,
Klieg lights clash
like barricades.

Children and lovers and soldiers and seers
laughed through tears
bright as cockades.
Dawnlight and darklight were one in their eyes,
full of surprise,
full of charades.

Gladly they sought where the balefires gleam.
There stood the dream,
banner-arrayed.
Little they thought that the bliss and the pain
heart and brain
ever betrayed.

Dream of a destiny simple as song,
What went wrong?
Where have you strayed?
Over a city the color of ash,
Klieg lights clash
like barricades.

About the Artists & Designers

Casey Chiappetta is an American University alumna who received her MS in Justice, Law, and Criminology in 2019 and her BA in Sociology in 2017. She is the recipient of the outstanding scholarship award at both the undergraduate and graduate levels, the first person to receive both prestigious awards. Casey currently works with The Pew Charitable Trusts. At Pew, she conducts research and manages research grants focused on making the civil legal system more equitable, open, and efficient. Prior, she worked at the National Legal Aid & Defender Association, providing technical assistance to civil legal aid and leading research on online dispute resolution. Her work has been published in: Disability & Society, Family Court Review, MIE Journal, among others.

LaShawn Whipple is an artist affiliated with the Prison Creative Arts Project. His cover art is entitled "The Oblivion."

Benjamin Feder an American University student currently pursuing a master's degree in Art History, with a focus on the Italian Renaissance. His experiences as both an artist and a student of art history are what initially compelled him to start a career in the art industry. Benjamin has worked in museums and galleries in both New York City and Washington D.C and is currently working in collections management. As an artist, Benjamin's favorite medium is clay, though he often includes mixed media into his sculptures.

Charlotte Lopez-Jauffret is a second-year doctoral student in Justice, Law & Criminology from American University. She received her Master of Forensic Science from the George Washington University in 2017. While obtaining her masters, she worked as a DNA technician at a private lab and later worked as a Forensic Intelligence Analyst in the public sector. By working both inside and outside of the lab, Charlotte strives to bridge the gap between science and the law.

Robert Johnson is a Professor of Justice, Law and Criminology at American University and Editor and Publisher of BleakHouse Publishing, which he founded in 2006. The press is devoted to publishing creative writing, art, and photography on social and criminal justice.

Other Titles from BleakHouse Publishing

Behind These Fences, E.L.

Pagan, John Corley

Silent, We Sit, Emily Dalgo

Black Bone, Alexa Marie Kelly

An Elegy for Old Terrors, Zoé Orfanos

Up the River, Chandra Bozelko

Distant Thunder, Charles Huckelbury

Enclosures: Reflections from the Prison Cell and the Hospital Bed, Shirin Karimi

A Zoo Near You, Robert Johnson et al.

Origami Heart: Poems by a Woman Doing Life, Erin George

Tales from the Purple Penguin, Charles Huckelbury

Burnt Offerings, Robert Johnson

Praise for Crass Casualties

What we all know - Anthony G. Amsterdam is the great Civil Rights attorney of our time. What many do not yet know – Tony is an equally masterful American poet. These narrative poems are fearlessly truthful and ferociously intelligent, sometimes tragic yet always exquisite, offering insights wide and deep that cross time and illuminate a vast array of subjects. The topical poems in Part 1 are about social justice, prisons, politics, history, and capital punishment. Especially, these are stories of the condemned and forgotten in a legal world that Tony knows, in a complete and nuanced way, better than anyone alive. Tony's sublime artistry is equally apparent in his "personal" poems – the meditations, travel poems, love poems and reflections in Part 2 of "Crass Casualties." Tony's voice is stunning and this work will endure. He is uniquely gifted - able to translate the wealth of professional and life-experiences into a poetics that speaks to us these days in ways that nobody has ever done before. These poems made me want to scream and cry and howl and – also – to cheer and applaud and smile with gratitude and admiration. Thanks, Tony. Your book is a lovely gift to us all.

Philip N. Meyer, Professor of Law, Vermont Law School and author of *Storytelling for Lawyers*

During his long career Anthony Amsterdam saved a great many people from the grotesque banality of state-sponsored execution, but, of course, not all of his death-row clients survived. Somehow, through all of this grimness and all of his legal pleadings, he managed to preserve his poetic soul. Reading Amsterdam's work is a revelation that might also give hope and pleasure to people who have never seen the inside of a jail and who never needed his services. The range – from the suffocating air of the penitentiary, to the restorative climate of the Scottish Highlands, to a brilliant glimpse of hidden Parisian life – is remarkable.

John R. MacArther, President & Publisher, *Harper's Magazine*

Crass Casualties by Anthony G. Amsterdam should be the next addition to the poetic pantheon's library. The work literally spans centuries and forms an essential bridge between those universal aesthetics that bind us to each other. This is a stunning confluence of erudition and talent, guiding the reader on an exploration of the individual's capacity for love, hope, and cruelty and how the proleptic nature of all three impacts the human condition. It is also an excursion into the sheer beauty and power of poetry, treating contemporary subjects (crime, prison) with the same mastery as he does sonnets and the deaths of van Gogh and Philip Sydney. In his poem, "The City's Passing," Amsterdam describes "[w]ords so potent, so superbly taut,/so eloquent with thought,/they could imprison/infinite, apocalyptic vision/in a single phrase." To which we can only add our thanks. The nod to Thomas Hardy aside, there is nothing even remotely crass about this impressive collection, and the only casualties are boredom and imposture.

Charles Huckelbury, former life-sentence prisoner
and author, *Distant Thunder*